Long before man arrived in the area, the landscape you see around you was formed by the action of the glacier which covered much of Upper Wharfedale during the last Ice Age, over 12,000 years ago.

As the climate became warmer and the ice receded, different plants and animals began to colonise the area.

Animals such as bears and reindeer roamed the area along with early man

Items found in Elbolton Cave, near Burnsall, indicate that in Neolithic times people had started to settle and carry out a primitive form of agriculture.

By the Iron Age, the Brigantes were using ploughs with metal blades and had established rough roads.

It was not until after the departure of the Romans that the Anglo Saxon settlers cleared trees in the valley bottoms for their farms and on the hillsides for terraced fields.

After millions of years Man, not nature, was beginning to have an effect on the landscape.

of Mercia.

Earl Edwin, who unsuccessfully courted William the Conqueror's daughter, was murdered by his own men. His land was granted to Robert de Rumilly who built Skipton Castle.

In 1120, Robert's daughter Cecily paid for Embsay Priory to be built for Black Canons of the Order of Saint Augustine. Such an act of generosity was often linked with the thought of ensuring a good place in the next life.

Embsay must have had drawbacks as, 35 years later, Cecily's daughter Alice offered the canons the sheltered site of Bolton.

Alice's daughter, also named Cecily, married the Earl of Albemarle whose family were benefactors of the Church and probably paid for the building of the Priory.

When the Albemarle line died out the Estate reverted to the Crown.

Boy of Egremont

Alice de Rumilly was said to have established the canons at Bolton as an expression of her grief for her son, the Boy of Egremont, who drowned in the Strid. An unlikely tale as the boy's signature appears on a document drawn up when the Priory was founded!

CLIFFORD
Lords of Skipton
Earls of Cumberland

In 1310 lands in Craven and at Barden were granted by Edward II to Robert Clifford, 1st Lord of Skipton and Earl Marshal of England.

After Henry VIII's Dissolution of the Monasteries, between 1536 and 1539, the greater share of the monastic estate was bought by Henry, 11th Lord of Skipton and 1st Earl of Cumberland, who was thought to have been brought up with the future Henry VIII.

This link with the Throne continued with the 1st Earl's grandson, George, the 3rd Earl, who commanded the *Elizabeth Bonadventure* against the Spanish Armada.

On the death of the 5th Earl in 1643 the Estate passed to his daughter Elizabeth who married Richard Boyle.

Lady Anne Clifford 1590-1676
The 3rd Earl's daughter, Lady Anne, outlived all male claimants and became 14th Lord of Skipton when she was 53. She married Richard Sackville, 3rd Earl of Dorset, and lived at Knole in Kent. Her second husband was Philip Herbert, 4th Earl of Pembroke. He employed Inigo Jones to work on their home, Wilton House.

DE RUMILLY

c.1190 First Skipton Castle built by Robert de Rumilly

1120 Cecily de Rumilly pays for Embsay Priory to be built

1155 Building of the Priory at Bolton commences

1273 Albemarle line dies out. Estate reverts to the Crown

1349-1350 Black Death

1455-1485 Wars of the Roses

CAVENDISH

c.1527-1608 Bess of Hardwick

1547 Bess marries Sir William Cavendish

1618 Bess of Hardwick's son, Sir William Cavendish, created Earl of Devonshire

1694 Wm. Cavendish, 4th Earl, created 1st Duke of Devonshire

1707-1729 William, 2nd Duke, *born 1673*

1729-1755 William, 3rd Duke, *born 1698*

1755-1764 William, 4th Duke, *born 1720*

CLIFFORD

1310 Land granted to Robert Clifford. 1st Lord of Skipton

1461 9th Lord, 'The Butcher Lord', forfeits land to the Crown

1485 Lands restored by Henry VII to 10th Lord, 'The Shepherd Lord'

1542 Monastic estate sold to Henry, 11th Lord and 1st Earl of Cumberland

1590 Lady Anne Clifford born

1613 Lady Elizabeth Clifford born
marries

1643 5th Earl dies

1688 Glorious Revolution: William & Mary come to throne

1707 Act of Union with Scotland

1745 Second Jacobite Rebellion. Bonnie Prince Charlie reaches Derby

marries

BOYLE

1566-1643 Richard, 1st Earl of Cork

1612-1697 Richard Boyle, 2nd Earl of Cork, created Earl of Burlington

1674-1703 Charles, 2nd Earl of Burlington

1695-1753 Richard, 3rd Earl of Burlington, the architect

1731-1754 Lady Charlotte Boyle

1066 Norman Invasion

1085-1086 Domesday Book

1154-1189 Reign of Henry II

1170 Thomas à Becket murdered

1215 Magna Carta

1314 Battle of Bannockburn

1318 & 1320 Raids by Scots force canons to flee

BOYLE
Earls of Cork and Burlington

Butcher Lord
John, 9th Lord of Skipton, 1430-1461, earned his nickname after his slaughter of Yorkists at the Battle of Wakefield during the Wars of the Roses.

Shepherd Lord
Henry, the 10th Lord, 1453-1524, gained his name after he sought refuge as a shepherd from his father's enemies. In 1513 he fought at the Battle of Flodden Field.

The great adventurer
George, 3rd Earl of Cumberland, 1558-1605 was Lady Anne Clifford's father and Champion to Elizabeth I.

The alchemist
Lady Margaret Russell, 1560-1616, married George, 3rd Earl of Cumberland. She discovered many new medicines and founded the almshouses at Beamsley.

Richard Boyle was the 2nd Earl of Cork and 1st Earl of Burlington. His grandson Richard, born in 1695 and usually referred to as Lord Burlington, became famous as an architect. His masterpieces include Burlington House (now the Royal Academy) and Chiswick Villa in London, and the Assembly Rooms at York.

Lismore Castle
Richard Boyle, 1st Earl of Cork, purchased Lismore Castle, in Ireland, from Sir Walter Raleigh.

Chiswick Villa
Section of the Villa
Lord Burlington employed William Kent to design the interior.

A keen collector, Lord Burlington managed to buy all the architectural designs of Inigo Jones and Palladio. These influenced his style and enriched the Devonshire Collections.

He was the patron and close friend of William Kent, originally a painter, who became a great architect, decorator and furniture designer. The aqueduct over the road, near the village green, is probably from a design by Kent.

In 1748 Lord Burlington's daughter, Lady Charlotte Boyle, born in 1731, married William Cavendish who became the 4th Duke of Devonshire.

The volume of a fixed mass of gas is inversely proportional to the pressure at a constant temperature

Boyle's Law
Robert Boyle, seventh son of the 1st Earl of Cork, was the scientist who propounded Boyle's Law in 1662. He also gave money which was used to build the Boyle School at Bolton Abbey, now the Rectory.

CAVENDISH

1766 Henry Cavendish proves hydrogen to be an element

1769-1770 Captain Cook's first voyage round the world

1775 James Watt develops his steam engine

1804 Trevithick's steam locomotive pulls 5 wagons and 70 passengers

1837 Queen Victoria's Coronation

1851 The Great Exhibition at Hyde Park

1867 Canada becomes first independent dominion in the Empire

1896 First motor cars appear on the road

1914-1918 First World War

1931 Great Depression; 3 million unemployed

1939-1945 Second World War

1952 Queen Elizabeth II comes to the throne

1959 Britain's first motorway built

1969 Neil Armstrong becomes the first man to set foot on the moon

1973 Britain joins the EEC

1994 Opening of the Channel Tunnel

1764-1811 William Cavendish, 5th Duke, *born 1748*

1811-1858 William Spencer Cavendish, 6th Duke, *born 1790*

1858-1891 William Cavendish, 7th Duke, *born 1808*

1891-1908 Spencer Compton Cavendish, 8th Duke, *born 1833*

1908-1938 Victor Cavendish, 9th Duke, *born 1868*

1938-1950 Edward Cavendish, 10th Duke, *born 1895*

1950- Andrew Cavendish, 11th Duke, *born 1920* m. Hon Deborah Mitford

Peregrine Cavendish, Marquess of Hartington, *born 1944* m. Amanda Heywood-Lonsdale

William Cavendish, Earl of Burlington, *born 1969*

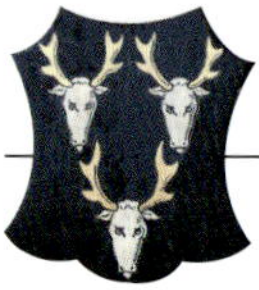

The Dukes of Devonshire
The 4th Duke's family was already well established at Chatsworth, Hardwick Hall and Devonshire House in London.

The 6th Duke

Lady Charlotte had made a good match in marrying the future **4th Duke of Devonshire**, whose family traced back to Bess of Hardwick. She could not be accused of marrying for money as she brought Burlington House, Chiswick Villa, Bolton Abbey, Londesborough Hall and Lismore Castle into the family. In addition there were Lord Burlington's architectural books and drawings, many paintings and the contents of the houses.

Sadly Charlotte died when she was only 23, having produced 4 children.

The 4th Duke served as Prime Minister from 1756 - 1757. His son William, the **5th Duke**, married Lady Georgiana Spencer who was famous for her charm, gambling debts and enormous hats.

At the age of 21, their son, the **6th Duke** inherited 8 houses and 200,000 acres of land. The 'Bachelor Duke' spent 47 years improving his estates, but his great extravagance forced him to sell some of his property in Yorkshire. Fortunately, he kept Bolton Abbey and employed Sir Joseph Paxton, who designed the Crystal Palace, to enlarge Bolton Hall.

Bess of Hardwick
c.1527-1608

In 1547 Bess married Sir William Cavendish, the second of her four husbands. She persuaded him to buy extensive property in Derbyshire, including the land on which Chatsworth was built. Her final masterpiece, Hardwick Hall, belonged to the family until 1959 when the Government took it in lieu of death duties.

CAVENDISH
Dukes of Devonshire

Georgiana, Duchess of Devonshire
Thomas Gainsborough (1728-1788)

The Rector of the time, the Reverend William Carr, apart from looking after his spiritual flock, was also the second largest agricultural tenant on the Estate. He and the Duke opened most of the Estate to the public and constructed 28 miles of footpaths. The arrival of the railway in 1888, established Bolton Abbey's position as a tourist destination.

Grandson of the 5th Duke's brother, the **7th Duke** was a devout man and responsible for the layout and pews of the Priory church. He founded the Cavendish Laboratory in Cambridge.

The **8th Duke**, a keen fisherman, was asked, and refused, three times to be Prime Minister.

The **9th Duke** loved politics and was Financial Secretary to the Treasury as well as Governor General of Canada. He enjoyed visiting Bolton Abbey for the grouse shooting, entertaining Edward VII and then George V at Bolton Hall.

The **10th Duke** continued the tradition of stewardship. At the age of 55, the Duke died suddenly while at his favourite occupation of chopping wood. Sadly, the Duke's eldest son William had been killed in action during the Second World War. This meant that his second son, Andrew, inherited the Dukedom along with 80% death duties on the estates and all the treasures that had been accumulated over four centuries.

The **11th Duke** is conscious of the need to look after the thousands of visitors who come to Bolton Abbey each year. A keen walker himself he has granted Open Access on the moors and opened up further footpaths, bringing the total to 80 miles. The Duke has seen the development of the Devonshire Arms Country House Hotel, the Devonshire Fell Hotel, the Cavendish Pavilion, a new Post Office and visitor centres.

The length of his tenure has enabled the Duke to see many of his plans come to fruition. Much thought has also gone into securing the long term preservation of the Estate. This will not only benefit all those whose livelihood depends upon it, but also all the visitors.

The 10th Duke

The wedding of the 10th Duke's son, William, to Kathleen Kennedy, sister of President John Kennedy. Sadly she was killed in aeroplane accident in 1948

The 11th Duke's son and family
From the left:
Earl of Burlington,
Alexander Carter,
Lady Celina Carter,
Lady Jasmine Cavendish,
Marchioness of Hartington
and Marquess of Hartington.

Bolton Abbey in the Olden Time
Sir Edwin Landseer (1802-1873)
The Lords of Skipton granted the Augustinian canons the carcass of every tenth beast killed in their forests. The canons were not encouraged to eat meat but their agricultural labourers and visitors had no such inhibitions!

Life in the Priory

The Black Canons' rules stipulated poverty, chastity and obedience. They were also to give alms, provide hospitality to visitors and serve as parish priests.

In the Priory's heyday, early in the 14th century, there were 26 canons and about 200 lay workers. The income required to live and to improve the Priory came from sheep farming, corn milling and revenue from the lead mines.

At 2am, the canons attended the first of seven services; the last being at 8pm. The first two services, Matins and Lauds, lasted most of the night and one of the canons would move around to check no one had fallen asleep.

The first meal was after midday and comprised bread and beer with some fish, vegetables and fruit. A small one course meal was taken after Vespers in the early evening.

Did you know?
The Estate today is responsible for 198 residential properties, 54 farms, 72 outlying barns and 27 commercial premises. 54 of these are listed buildings. It employs more than 150 people and supports a community of over 1,500 people.

The Nave
Today the 13th century nave, with its magnificent ceiling and stained glass windows by Augustus Pugin, serves as the parish church.

The West Tower
Started in 1520 but never finished because of the Dissolution of the Monasteries in 1539. The tower is only partly connected to the beautiful 13th century west front which it would have replaced.

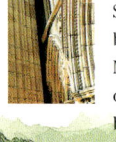

Bolton Hall
The tower incorporates the original arched entrance to the Priory. The first substantial enlargement was made by the Cliffords and in the 1840s it was further enlarged by Sir Joseph Paxton, who later designed the Crystal Palace for the Great Exhibition in London.

Chapter House (Meetings)
Dorter (Sleeping above Common Room)
Cloister
Cellarium (Storage)
Frater or Refectory (Eating)
Kitchen

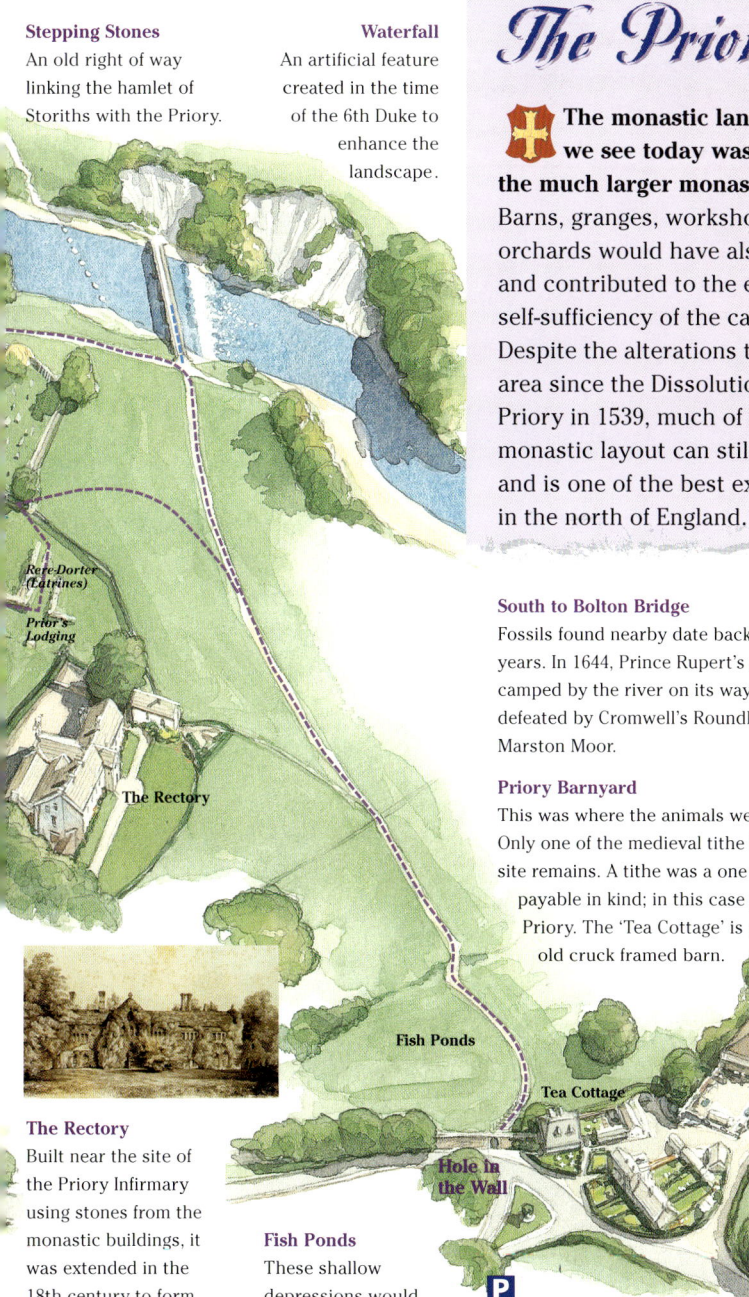

Stepping Stones
An old right of way linking the hamlet of Storiths with the Priory.

Waterfall
An artificial feature created in the time of the 6th Duke to enhance the landscape.

The Priory

The monastic landscape we see today was part of the much larger monastic estate. Barns, granges, workshops and orchards would have also existed and contributed to the economic self-sufficiency of the canons. Despite the alterations to this area since the Dissolution of the Priory in 1539, much of the monastic layout can still be seen and is one of the best examples in the north of England.

South to Bolton Bridge
Fossils found nearby date back 330 million years. In 1644, Prince Rupert's army camped by the river on its way to being defeated by Cromwell's Roundheads at Marston Moor.

Priory Barnyard
This was where the animals were kept. Only one of the medieval tithe barns on the site remains. A tithe was a one tenth tax payable in kind; in this case paid to the Priory. The 'Tea Cottage' is part of an old cruck framed barn.

Rere-Dorter (Latrines)
Prior's Lodging
The Rectory
Fish Ponds
Tea Cottage
Tithe Barn
Hole in the Wall

The Rectory
Built near the site of the Priory Infirmary using stones from the monastic buildings, it was extended in the 18th century to form the Free School of the Hon. Robert Boyle. In 1875 it merged with the Petyt School and the building became the Rectory.

Fish Ponds
These shallow depressions would probably have held water either to hold fish for the table or to make ice.

The de Rumilly Walk

Start	Village car park
Distance	1 mile / 1.6 km
Time	Allow 1 hour
Terrain	Easy, some steps
Pushchairs	Yes
Wheelchairs	Yes, via Priory drive
Dogs	On leads

A Year by the river

SPRING

The Wharfe is one of the most famous trout and grayling rivers in the North of England. Before the trout season opens on 25 March there is much to be done, such as clearing the river banks of debris brought down by the winter floods. Control of vermin such as mink and rats is crucial, especially with the return of migratory birds to nest.

SUMMER

With the lower water levels at this time of year the bailiff needs to check for pollution, as well as keeping an eye out for poachers. The type of insects hatching on the river changes as the day goes on; anglers need to be kept informed so they can alter their fishing flies accordingly.

AUTUMN

This is when trout spawn and they must be able to reach the spawning becks that run into the Wharfe. Blockages are cleared and a few trout are caught and checked for disease before being returned to the river. The grayling season continues on until 28 February but trout fishing ends on 30 September.

WINTER

With the trout out of the way up the spawning becks, the bailiff is able to assess the numbers and distribution of grayling in the river.

Did you know?
The Estate cares for seven miles of river and 80 miles of footpaths.

Look out for:

SPRING
*Dippers
Goosanders
Herons
Kingfishers
Mallard
Moorhens
Sand martins
Sandpipers
Wagtails*

SUMMER
*Dippers
Goosanders
Herons
Kingfishers
Pied wagtails
Sand martins
Sandpipers
Swallows
Gold ringed dragonflies*

AUTUMN
*Oyster catchers
Pied flycatchers
Sand martins
Spotted flycatchers
Warblers*

WINTER
*Canada geese
Goldeneye
Mallard*

Royalty also arrived by train.
George V is met by the 9th Duke of Devonshire at Bolton Abbey Station.

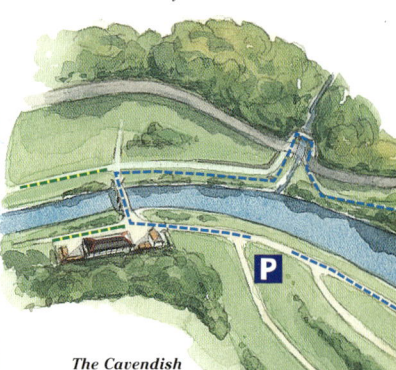

The Cavendish Pavilion
The exterior today and the interior as it was in the 1920s.

Cavendish Pavilion

Recently enlarged, the Pavilion serves meals and refreshments. It was originally built in the 1890s as a tea room for the thousands of day visitors who arrived by train. Wagonettes brought them from Bolton Abbey Station. Today you can still travel to Bolton Abbey Station from Embsay on steam trains run by the Embsay and Bolton Abbey Steam Railway.

An inspirational landscape

This riverside walk encompasses the heart of the romantic landscape which inspired some of our great artists and poets. Wordsworth, Turner, Girtin and Landseer were some of those who captured the beauty of the place in words and paint. Little has changed over the centuries; the cattle still come to drink from the river opposite the Priory.

A view of Bolton Abbey
George Cuitt (1743-1818)

To Storiths

The Cavendish Memorial Fountain was built to commemorate Lord Frederick, 2nd son of the 7th Duke, who was assassinated in Phoenix Park, Dublin, 12 hours after his arrival as Chief Secretary to Ireland in 1882.

The Cavendish Walk

Start	Sandholme car park
Distance	2 miles / 3 km
Time	Allow 1 hour
Terrain	Moderate
Pushchairs	Possible, 3 stiles.
Wheelchairs	No
Dogs	On leads

Strid Wood

Strid Wood contains the largest area of acidic oak woodland in the Yorkshire Dales. Being an upland site Strid Wood favours the native **sessile oak**, which can be identified by the lack of a stalk supporting the acorns. Unlike the English, or pedunculate oak, the **sessile oak** can thrive on the wetter, less fertile acidic soils of the area.

Strid Wood's position in a steep gorge made it unsuitable as farmland and so protected it from the tree clearances which occurred on the surrounding land.

Within a relatively small area the mixture of mature and young trees, hardwoods and conifers provides an ideal habitat for a rich variety of birds, plants, animals and insects. The river Wharfe flowing through the wood adds to the number and diversity of habitats. In a short distance the river changes character from the fearsome Strid to deep still waters and again to wide rushing shallows further down. The banks provide a corridor for the movement of animals.

Did you know?
The Estate cares for five Sites of Special Scientific Interest (SSSIs).

The Laund Oak
is thought to be over 600 years old. In the past oak from Strid Wood was used for the Priory, the Tithe Barn and the bridge at the Cavendish Pavilion.

In the 16th century the Forests of Barden and Knaresborough met here at the river Wharfe. It was said that a squirrel could go from Knaresborough to Skipton without touching the ground!

Cumberland Trail
Starting from Strid Wood car park this easy nature trail winds through the wood with resting places and a viewing platform overlooking Barden Beck. Cartoons and exhibits on the trail tell the story of the wood and its wildlife.
A bird hide provides excellent opportunities to look at the birds and animals.

The Strid
is extremely dangerous because of its depth, force of water and the undercurrents that hold anything that goes in under water for several days.

Strid Barn
An exhibition explores life in Strid Wood. During the nesting season a video link shows live action from a nest.

Great upheavals

✠ **In 1810 William Carr, the Rector, obtained the consent of the 6th Duke of Devonshire to open up Strid Wood to the public.** Today you can follow his paths and enjoy the views from his carefully placed seats, just as William Wordsworth did. However this tranquil landscape was not always peaceful because it was formed by massive geological upheavals; some of the rocks date back over 300 million years.

The Strid in 1893
S.L.Booth

The Strid

was formed by the wearing away of softer rock by the circular motion of small stones in hollows, forming a series of potholes which in time linked together to form a deep, water-filled, chasm.

Lud Islands

300 million years ago, when the area was covered by sea, the rocks of Wharfedale were deposited as sediments on the sea bed. These limestone deposits, made from the shells of marine animals, are now covered by coarse sandstone layers.

Across the river and south of Lud Islands is an outcrop of highly folded rocks. Originally these were horizontal layers of limestone and shale but over millions of years they were compressed, probably by the movements of the nearby fault line.

The Egremont Walk

Start	Sandholme car park
Distance	4 miles / 6.4 km
Time	Allow 2 hours
Terrain	Moderate
Pushchairs	Up to the Strid
Wheelchairs	Up to the Strid
Dogs	On leads

The Farmer's Year

SPRING
Lambing starts at the beginning of April. Dairy cattle are turned out to grass in May. Before the animals go out fences and walls have to be checked and repaired.

SUMMER
The cows are usually brought in for milking twice a day and calves have to be fed morning and night. The hill sheep, Swaledales and Dalesbred, are turned onto the moors to graze. The cross-bred sheep, which produce their lambs earlier than the hill sheep, are kept in the fields. Sheep shearing takes place in June and the meadows are cut for hay and silage, which provides feed for the animals during the winter.

AUTUMN
Rams (tups) are introduced to the ewes to produce next year's lambs. Surplus sheep and cattle are taken to the sales.

WINTER
When the temperature drops and the land is wet the cattle are brought inside. In the worst weather the hill sheep are brought down off the moors and additional feeding with hay may be necessary during very bad weather.
On the dairy farms the twice daily routine of milking continues. The buildings have to be 'mucked out' and the manure, or slurry, is stored in middens in preparation for spreading on the land next spring.

Did you know?
The Estate farms produce about 10,000,000 litres of milk every year.

Barden Tower
Atkinson Grimshaw (1836-1893)

Barden Bridge
This beautiful bridge with its impressive cutwaters was built in 1659 and repaired in 1676, after a flood which destroyed six bridges over the Wharfe.

Family businesses
In the 17th century the inhabitants became tenants with strict leases often favouring the interests of the landowner. Many farms have remained in the same family over the generations and the same names can be traced over several centuries. Farm books such as Ralph Stott's of Drebley, dating back to 1823, provide a fascinating insight into life at the time.

The Tower and its setting

Henry Clifford, 10th Lord, developed the landscape around Barden Tower. It stood in the Little Park, with fishponds and barns beyond. Across the river, Coney Warren provided rabbits for fresh meat; its curved wall is still visible. To the west, and including Lower Barden Reservoir, is the deer park named the Great or Broad Park, first enclosed by Henry Clifford with a wooden fence and later walled by Lady Anne Clifford. In the past there have been a school, two chapels and an inn at Barden.

Aqueduct

The splendid castellations hide the pipe that carries water from the reservoirs at the top of Nidderdale to the cities of West Yorkshire.

The hunting forest

The Forest of Barden was granted to Robert de Rumilly by William the Conqueror.

In 1310, when Robert Clifford became 1st Lord of Skipton, Barden was a hunting forest with 6 lodges: Barden, Drebley, Howgill, Laund, Gamsworth and Ungaine. 'Forest' is a legal term meaning, like Royal forests, it was subject to its own laws. These were enforced by officials and courts to safeguard its resources: game, pasture, timber, minerals, peat and natural products such as honey.

There were large areas of heath and scrub, as well as woodland. Lodges initially housed the lord's officers, but in the 14th century, with the exception of Barden, they were leased as cattle farms.

Barden Tower

In the late 15th century, Henry Clifford, 'The Shepherd Lord', rebuilt the hunting lodge at Barden in stone and made it his principal residence. The area was liable to raids by the Scots so its defensive position, commanding the river crossing, was advantageous. In 1515, he built the Priest's House next to the Chapel.

In 1659, Lady Anne Clifford restored Barden Tower, although in fact it belonged to another branch of the family. Following her death it was taken over by its rightful owners the Earls of Cork, but sadly fell into decline in the late 18th century.

The Clifford Walk

Start	Strid car park
Distance	2½ miles / 4km
Time	Allow 1½ hours
Terrain	Moderate
Pushchairs	Possible, 10 stiles
Wheelchairs	No
Dogs	On leads

The woodland year

SPRING
After a long winter, the trees burst into leaf forcing the young trees and weeds below to compete for light and nutrients. Foresters start weeding the commercial plantations and the trees are checked for weevil and rabbit damage.

SUMMER
Weeding continues in the young plantations and preparations for the coming planting season start in the areas of woodland which have been felled. Work undertaken includes fencing against rabbits and maintenance of drainage ditches.

AUTUMN
Harvesting the timber by felling in selected areas can begin. The planting season also gets under way with an average of 20,000 trees planted every year.

WINTER
Tree planting continues throughout the winter when the weather permits. Thinning and clear-felling is in full swing when the ground is hard with frost, making it easier to extract the timber. Rabbit and squirrel control is necessary towards spring as they kill young trees.

Timber extraction, Strid Wood, 1929.

Did you know?
The Estate gathers up to 8,000 acorns each year for future planting.

Look out for:

SPRING
Bluebells
Dog's mercury
Wild garlic
Wood anemones
Wood sorrel
Blackcaps
Wood warblers
Green veined white & orange tip butterflies

SUMMER
Bugle
Rosebay and Great hairy willow herbs
Wood avens
Yarrow
Yellow pimpernel
Small tortoiseshell, peacock & wall brown butterflies
2 & 7 spot ladybirds

AUTUMN
Chicken of the woods
Death cap
Fly agaric
Stinkhorn
Herons
Pheasants
Wrens
Roe deer

WINTER
Bramblings
Fieldfare
Great spotted woodpeckers
Kestrels
Little owls
Redwings
Tawny owls
Sparrowhawks
Roe deer

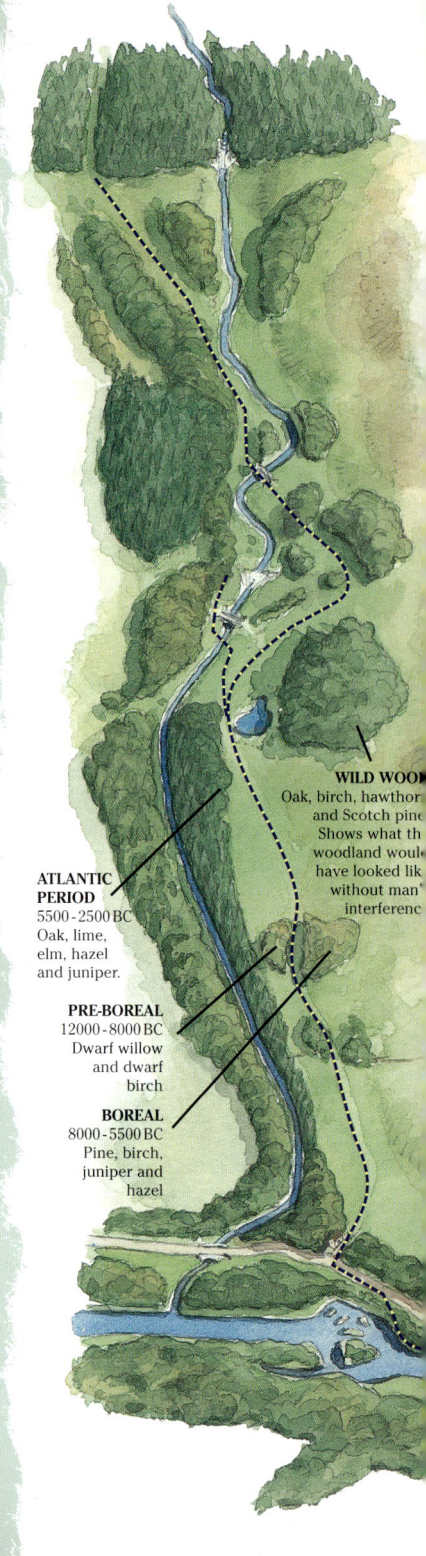

WILD WOOD
Oak, birch, hawthorn and Scotch pine
Shows what the woodland would have looked like without man's interference

ATLANTIC PERIOD
5500 - 2500 BC
Oak, lime, elm, hazel and juniper.

PRE-BOREAL
12000 - 8000 BC
Dwarf willow and dwarf birch

BOREAL
8000 - 5500 BC
Pine, birch, juniper and hazel

The Valley of Desolation

Tucked away above the Low Park lies a picturesque valley where Posforth Gill drops 17 metres over a spectacular waterfall. The valley owes its dramatic name to the desolation caused by a tremendous storm in 1826. Nature has long since repaired the devastation and the area is now subject to new plantings and interpretation that explains the formation of the landscape since the last Ice Age and shows the succession of plants and trees as the surroundings changed.

The 6th Duke, Mr Beaumont and Burgoyne, the Duke's Gamekeeper, 1812.
Ramsay Richard Reinagle (1775-1862)

A constantly changing landscape

During the last Ice Age, the valley of Posforth Gill would have been covered with a glacier. When the ice finally retreated glacial action had widened and lowered the valley floor. Since then the waters in the gill have further deepened the valley creating waterfalls. Mosses and lichens growing in the tundra conditions after the Ice Age were succeeded by dwarf willow and birch and in time forests formed. These were cleared by Iron Age man and his descendants and as a consequence the upland areas reverted to moorland. The land form is still changing with landslips as recent as 25 years ago.

The Waterfall
Since the last Ice Age erosion by water flowing down the gill has caused the waterfall to retreat gradually from the riverbank, leaving a steep sided valley below the fall.

Holly
Before you enter Low Park you will notice the large number of holly trees. The smooth leaved young growth used to be fed to deer and stock as winter fodder.

Simon's Seat
Continuing on from the Valley of Desolation the energetic walker can cross the moor to Simon's Seat, a rocky outcrop 385m above the river with spectacular views all round. The name is thought to relate to the Simon Magi - Druidic magicians who followed Simon Magus, claimed to be one of The Three Wise Men. The Britons and Romans held him in superstitious awe.

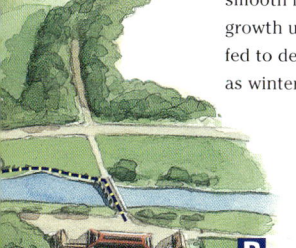

Cavendish Pavilion

The Duke's Walk

Start	Sandholme car park
Distance	3 miles / 5 km return
Time	Allow 1½ hours
Terrain	Moderate / hard
Pushchairs	No
Wheelchairs	No
Dogs	No

Swathes of purple

Returning from the moors, 1930s.
From the left: William, the late Lord Hartington; his brother Andrew, the 11th Duke; the 10th Duke; Lady Elizabeth and Lady Anne Cavendish.

The moorland year

SPRING

When the grouse and other moorland birds are nesting the predators - foxes, stoats, carrion crows and magpies - need to be controlled.

SUMMER

Long dry days bring the danger of fire. A careless match can cause such devastation to the rich variety of birds, animals and plants living amongst the heather that the Yorkshire Dales National Park sometimes has to close the moors to protect them. On one weekend gamekeepers had to cope with 40 incidents of loose dogs causing havoc to the sheep and the wildlife. Late July and August is when control of the ever encroaching bracken takes place. As the 'Glorious 12th' of August approaches the gamekeepers prepare for the grouse season by repairing shooting butts and roads.

AUTUMN

When the grouse season finishes the gamekeepers start to burn small areas of the heather to create a patchwork of different aged plants. This provides nesting sites and shelter in the taller, older plants and food from the shoots of the young heather.

WINTER

Heather burning continues along with other moorland management tasks - such as the control of foxes and stoats - to maintain the ideal habitat for upland birds and sheep.

Look out for:

SPRING
Blackheaded gulls
Canada geese
Curlews
Golden plovers
Lapwings
Meadow pipits
Merlins
Redshank
Snipe

SUMMER & AUTUMN
Curlews
Golden plovers
Grouse
Lapwings
Merlins

WINTER
Grouse
Sparrowhawks

Right: Excerpt from the game book of 1911. The King was George V and his host was the 9th Duke.

In late summer, the hills become cloaked in purple as the heather blooms. The bell heather is the first to appear followed by ling heather.

The Estate has seen grouse shooting over its moors since the 1750s. The gamebooks record the numbers shot by such illustrious guests as Edward VII and George V. The stewardship of the moors has ensured the survival of the heather. Without grazing sheep, trees would naturally regenerate. The control of predators not only protects the red grouse, but also the merlin and upland waders, such as curlews and snipe.

In 1968 an Access Agreement gave access to over almost 14,000 acres of open moorland. Numerous upland paths enable the public to enjoy this wild, spectacular country.

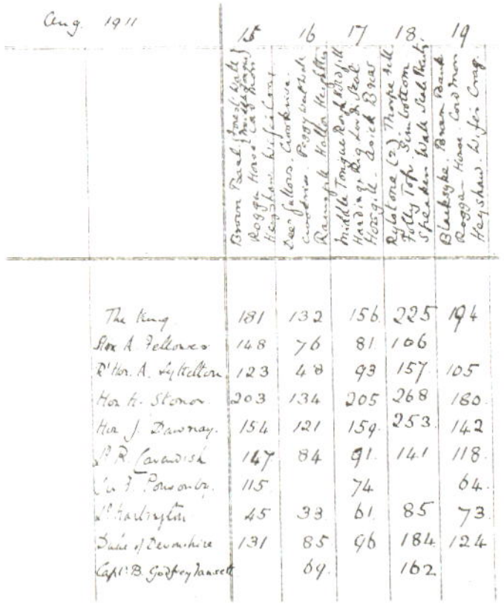